the ELF off the SHELF

A Christmas Tradition Gone Bad

D1161705

The Elf off the Shelf as told to Brendan O'Neill by Horace the Elf.

Copyright © 2011 by F+W Media, Inc.

All rights reserved.
This book, or parts thereof, may not be reproduced in any form without permission from the publisher; exceptions are made for brief excerpts used in published reviews.

Published by Adams Media, a division of F+W Media, Inc.
57 Littlefield Street, Avon, MA 02322. U.S.A.
www.adamsmedia.com

ISBN 10: 1-4405-2791-1
ISBN 13: 978-1-4405-2791-3
eISBN 10: 1-4405-2839-X
eISBN 13: 978-1-4405-2839-2

Printed in China.

10   9   8   7   6   5   4   3   2   1

Library of Congress Cataloging-in-Publication Data
is available from the publisher.

This book is a parody and has not been prepared, approved, or authorized by the author or publisher of *The Elf on the Shelf* children's book. *The Elf on the Shelf* is a registered trademark of CCA and B, LLC.

Many of the designations used by manufacturers and sellers to distinguish their product are claimed as trademarks. Where those designations appear in this book and Adams Media was aware of a trademark claim, the designations have been printed with initial capital letters.

Art Direction, Frank Rivera and Karen Cooper.
Photos by Joe Ciarcia, Symphony Photography.

*This book is available at quantity discounts for bulk purchases.
For information, please call 1-800-289-0963.*

the ELF off the SHELF

A Christmas Tradition Gone Bad

Written (and Caused) by Horace the Elf

A new holiday parody—for Mom and Dad!

Avon, Massachusetts

Around Christmastime every year,
Santa sends out elves to see what they can hear.
They help him decide who's Naughty and Nice,
And he bases his list off their advice.

Your mom went out and found quite the deal.
75% off? Now that's a steal!
I can't wait to go from the box to the shelf
And make Santa proud of this discount elf.

On my very first day out of the box
You must find me a name that totally rocks.
What will it be? Something awesomely rad?
Like E. Diddy, Elf: The Naughty Hunter, or Brad?

Whichever you pick
I hope it's cool.
There's nothing worse
Than looking like a tool.

E. DIDDY

Elf: The Naughty Hunter

THE NOTORIOUS E.L.F.

The Artist Formerly Known as ELF

BRAD

It'd be such a shame
To see your name on the wrong list
Just 'cause your bad choice,
Well, got me pissed.

So I've left it in your hands
And what did you decide?
Horace the Elf? Are you serious?
I could cry.

A travesty. A tragedy.
A complete and major bomb.
This is not what I was thinking
When I came home with your mom.

But the decision's been made
In multi-color crayon.
Looks like there's nothing to do
But take it like a man . . .

. . . Er elf, you know what I'm saying.
I'm really upset—not even playing.
While my name can't change, my attitude can.
Be a good elf? *Horace* isn't following *that* plan.

The _Adams_ family would like to welcome our elf, **HORACE**.

I might be stuck with this name,
But I won't be stuck in one spot.
Once you all fall asleep,
I'll have fun without getting caught.

In the dark I'll come down
From whichever spot I've been placed,
And spend the wee hours
Making up for the boring days.

Like with tonight's party,
Aunt Sue brought a pie,
And Dad spiked the eggnog,
Which I wanted to try.

But while the guests were here,
I could only sit and listen.
Now that everyone's gone . . .
I can let loose and dig in.

One glass became two
And two became four.
The next thing I knew,
The ceiling was the floor.

As things started spinning,
I saw this lil' guy,
Hanging high in the tree
So I thought I'd stop by.

We got to talking
About life in the tree
And that's when I found out,
He's got an even worse job than me!

Shoving nuts in your mouth?
You've got to be joking.
Buddy, your career choice . . .
What the *heck* were you smoking?

Hanging out with my new pal
Actually got me to thinking.
(That is, once my hangover kicked
And my ears stopped ringing.)

Sure, my name isn't the greatest fit,
But I'm trying my best to live with it.
And even though I've been *this close* to snapping,
It beats the Workshop's hammering and wrapping.

After all, these kids need me
Much more than I need them.
If they want their holiday to be merry,
They better listen to this new poem:

'Tis the week before Christmas
And all through the house
Either be nice to Horace,
Or be on the outs.

Ugh. Really? Seriously?
This is the end of that.
I give them another chance,
And I wind up a toy for their cat?

Yeah, the cat's the reason I'm here,
But Mom, Dad, and the kids definitely aren't in the clear.
Through breakfast, lunch, and dinner I had to stay
Lying behind the can—the *entire* frickin' day!

These people clearly don't care.
They're not even trying.
If I don't matter to them,
I'll look to someone else I've been eying.

She's a real doll,
If I say so myself.
Better than anything else
I'd find on the shelf.

And tonight's the night
I'm going to make my move,
Especially since her boyfriend Ken
Is at their dream house in Malibu.

If I'm going to be going,
I'm going out with a bang.
Forget being just an elf on the shelf,
This elf's got too much game.

Who would've thought she'd be such a prude.
Rejected by Barbie? Are you serious, dude?
Frustrated and irritated, dejected and denied,
Enough is enough. That's it, you guys.

I thought this gig would be a nice change of pace,
Yet it's been nothing but trouble since I came to this place.
But I was sent down here with a job to do,
And I'm going to do it, regardless of you.

I said I'd deliver your list up north to the Pole
And even after all this, that is still my goal.
So on Christmas morning there'll be gifts under the tree,
Though now there's got to be something in it for me.

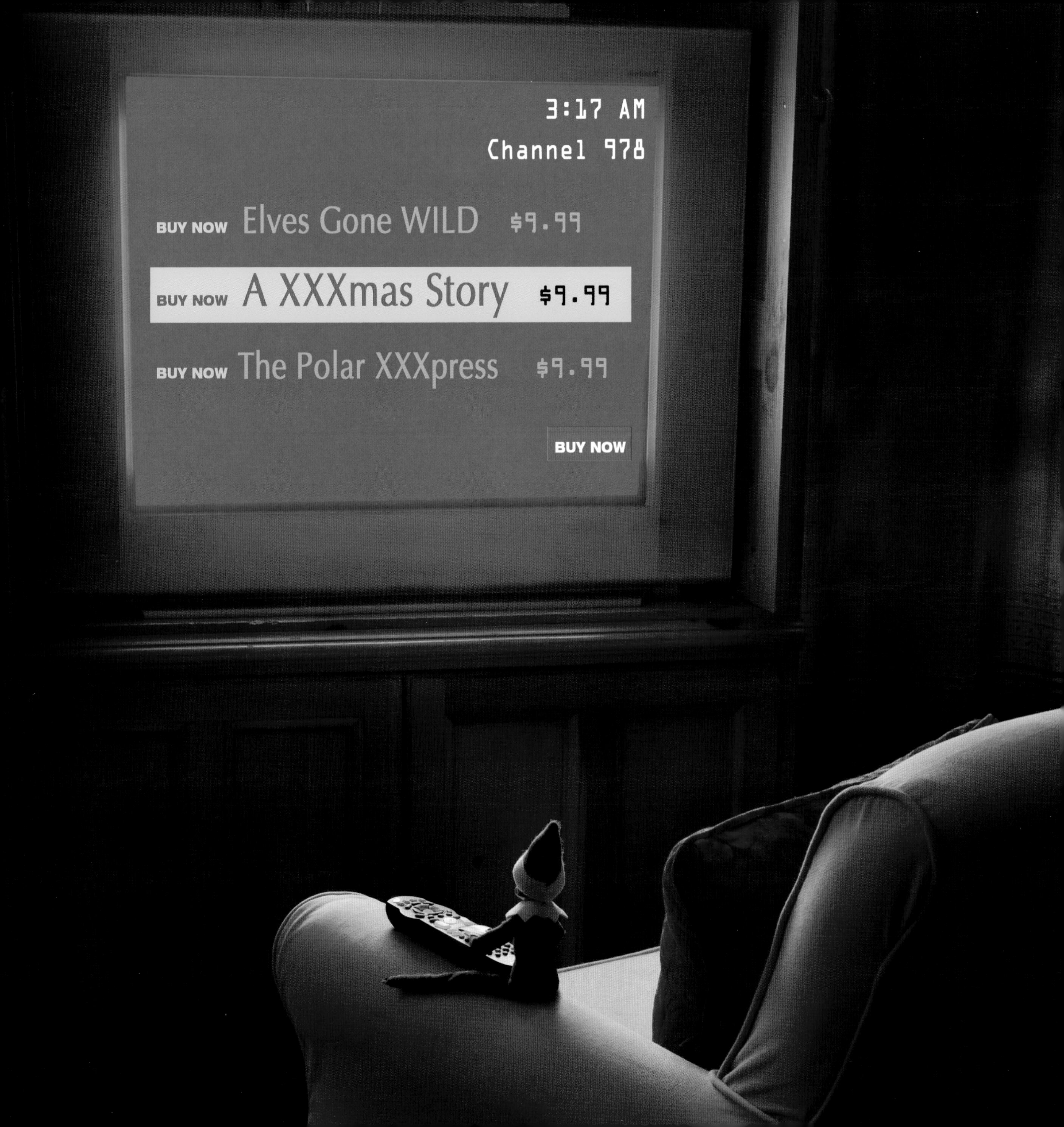
3:17 AM
Channel 978
BUY NOW Elves Gone WILD $9.99
BUY NOW A XXXmas Story $9.99
BUY NOW The Polar XXXpress $9.99
BUY NOW

Let's take a look and see what you've written
To figure out exactly what I'll be given.
A ball? A doll? A dumb toy train?
Come on. Year after year it's always the same.

Forget the ball . . . and the doll . . .
And that stupid toy train.
Let's go with gift cards and cash,
And that sweet new zombie videogame.

A little for you, a little more for me.
Finally! Something on which we can all agree.
With this wrapped up, it's time for me to go.
Upward and onward and out of here to the North Pole.

Except the last magic sleigh
Rode away without me.
So it's either hitch it or hoof it,
If the North Pole's where I want to be.

On Dodge! On Lancer! On Prius, or Pickup!
On Camaro! On Contour! On Durango, or Civic!
I'll find a ride and deliver your list,
Even though I'm still kind of pissed.

But hey! With this snow coming down
It may still be a merry, white Christmas
With sledding and caroling and mistletoe kisses.
Huh . . . maybe I will miss this . . .

Get away from it all
TROPICAL TRAVELS

NORTH POLE OR BUST!!

Forget it! I'm bailing!
This job's for the birds.
I'm an elf, not Frosty.
This crap's beyond words.

I tried to do my job.
I actually, truly did.
But it was all too much,
I'm really sorry, kids.

First that awful, awful name,
And then all the disrespect,
Hanging drunk from the tree,
And being batted around by your pet?

No thank you. Peace out.
I'm seriously exhausted.
Frostbite's my limit,
And, look, we've crossed it.

Forget Santa's Workshop in the freezing cold.
I'm sick and tired of doing what I'm told.
Instead I headed south to enjoy the surf and the sand,
Catch some rays and get myself a tan.

Now, the only shelf that matters to me
Is the top one where all the tequila will be.
So Feliz Navidad, and Happy New Year,
I wish I could say, I wish you were here.

POSTAL SERVICE

TO: MR. CLAUS
From: HORACE

SANTA CLAUS
1 REINDEER LANE
NORTH POLE

Before you get worked up and start to fret,
I mailed your list, so don't be upset.
I sent it first class (on my own dime),
So I'm *sure* Santa got it in time . . .

Christmas morning will be such a surprise
When you wake up, you won't believe your eyes.
I almost wish I could be there myself,
Just to show everyone that I'm a good elf.

But I'll be spending the day relaxing down here.
Who knows? Maybe I'll see you again next year . . .

The _____

family would

like to welcome

our elf, _____.